The Bible of Lost Pets

JAMEY DUNHAM was born and raised in Dayton, Ohio. He attended college at Miami University in Oxford, Ohio and received an MFA from Bennington College in Bennington, Vermont. He is currently an Associate Professor of English at Sinclair Community College in Dayton, Ohio where he serves as Editor of the literary journal *Flights*. Jamey's award-winning prose poems have been published widely in many distinguished journals and appear in several anthologies including *The Best American Poetry 2005* (Scribner, 2005) and *Great American Prose Poems: From Poe to the Present* (Scribner, 2003). He is also the co-editor of the textbook anthology *An Introduction to the Prose Poem* (Firewheel Editions, 2009). Jamey lives in Cincinnati, Ohio, with his wife and their son and daughter. *The Bible of Lost Pets*, which was one of the inaugural winners of the Crashaw Prize, is his first collection.

The Bible of Lost Pets

Jamey Dunham

SALT

Cambridge

PUBLISHED BY SALT PUBLISHING
14a High Street, Fulbourn, Cambridge CB21 5DH United Kingdom

© Jamey Dunham 2009

The right of Jamey Dunham to be identified as the
author of this work has been asserted by him in accordance
with Section 77 of the Copyright, Designs and Patents Act 1988.

Salt Publishing 2009

Printed and bound in the United Kingdom by the MPG Books Group

Typeset in Swift 9.5 / 13

ISBN 978 1 84471 563 3 hardback
ISBN 978 1 84471 ??? ? paperback

Salt Publishing Ltd gratefully acknowledges
the financial assistance of Arts Council England

1 3 5 7 9 8 6 4 2

for Laur, Sam and Zoey

Contents

Acknowledgments

Grateful acknowledgement is made to the following journals where some of these poems first appeared: *Alembic, Another Chicago Magazine, BOMB Magazine, Boston Review, Boulevard, The Cincinnati Review, Connecticut Review, Double Room, Fence, Free Lunch, In Posse Review, The Iowa Review, Key Satch (el), Lit, Maelstrom, Margie, Mid-American Review, Paragraph, Pith, Quarterly West, Salt Hill, Sentence, Tarpaulin Sky* and *Third Coast.*

In addition, poems appeared in the following anthologies: "An American Story" appeared in the *Great American Prose Poems: From Poe to the Present* (Scribner, 2003), "Urban Myth" appeared in *The Best American Poetry 2005* (Scribner, 2005), "The Neighbor's Dog" appeared in the *PP/FF: An Anthology* (Starcherone Books, 2006), "Urban Myth," and "Poem with Weasels, ca. 1930s (Black and White)," appeared in *An Introduction to the Prose Poem* (Firewheel Editions, 2009) and "Magpies and Orphans" appeared in *Online Writing: The Best of the First Ten Years* (Snow*Vigate Press, 2009).

The author would like to express his sincere gratitude to his wife Laurie and their children Sam and Zoey for their constant love and support. He would also like to thank Lee and Debby Dunham and Lynley Culpepper for years of understanding and encouragement. Finally, this book would not be possible were it not for the generosity and kindness of James Reiss, David Lehman, Peter Johnson, Brian Clements, Chris Hamilton-Emery, Jen Hamilton-Emery and the many Editors of the journals, magazines and anthologies where these poems first appeared. Thank you.

Part One

Prairie Dog Town

I AM THE LAST black-footed ferret in this prairie dog town. I have a striped wool sock slung through my belt loop and a black toy mask over my eyes. As I nose my way down the street I toss a dime in a blind man's cup and suddenly all eyes are on me. People everywhere begin pointing at me and barking in high-pitched chirps. I run to the curb but the cabs won't stop, they barrel past like buffalo with their heads between their fenders. By now the barking is deafening. People are leaning out of windows and popping up through manholes just to chime in. I race around the corner and duck into an alley. A coyote crouching in the shadows over a dead chicken, casually stands up and lights a cigarette. Says he thought my kind was extinct.

Go West

I HIT A RACCOON driving home from work the other night. At first I thought I blew a tire but then I caught its yellow eyes in the mirror. I turned the car around and drove back to take a look. When I saw the poor thing splayed out in the road, I knew what I had to do. I took the raccoon home and placed it in my Mother's bed. I hadn't been in her room in years. The sheets were stiff and cold as I drew them back. I sat in the wicker chair in the corner and watched it lying there, breathing hard. Something about the raccoon fit with the room. The eyes that seemed so alive on the road were different now, seemed to reflect more light than they held. I got up from the chair and paced the hall. Each time I passed the door I could feel the raccoon's eyes following me. Finally, I crossed the floor to where the raccoon lay. I knew what I had to do. As I opened the door to the garage, I thought of all the suffering that could have been avoided. I turned on the ignition, closed the door and walked to the end of the driveway. I lay down on the cold asphalt and for the first time in a long time I thought of my Mother. I heard the car shift into gear and closed my eyes. The car rolled down the driveway, veered to avoid hitting me, and pulled into the street. I opened my eyes and watched as the car proceeded to the corner, turned and disappeared in the direction of the city. I closed my eyes again. I thought of the raccoon on the open road. Maybe it wouldn't stop at the city, maybe it would keep going, head west. I thought about the mountains, and the ocean rising up between them. I thought of marvelous sunsets bruising the sky, like the ones on the postcards from my Mother. I thought about what it was that held some people to the ground, while others passed overhead like satellites. I thought about that for a long time before I finally got up and went back in the house.

A Prayer for Slow-Poke Jackass

THE SHERIFF WAS BEAT. It had been a long crusade and still the west was uninhibited. He led his horse to the hitching post, then stopped, bowed deeply from the waist, and set it free. "Adieu," he said waving his pistol as the horse trotted off. Then he changed his mind and began chasing after it, cursing and spitting, finally giving up and shooting it in front of the orphanage. The children playing outside clapped and cheered, but the Sheriff shook his head and headed into the saloon for a drink.

An old prospector seated in the corner was selling tumble-weeds for a nickel. "They're perfect," he said, hoarding them like sheep. The Sheriff saddled up to the bar and ordered a whiskey. A few seats down the Lone Ranger was perched on a stool, anxiously peeking around from behind his mask and milking a tall glass of milk. He was waiting to meet with a representative of the Silver Bullet Suppository Company. "I felt like a whore," he would later confide to a companion who was not Tonto but whose strong silence must have offered some support.

The Sheriff finished his drink and pushed away from the bar. He took one last look at the sorry crowd and headed back into the street. Down the road the orphans were chasing horse flies from the carcass of the dead horse. They were collecting them in mason jars like fireflies. The Sheriff sat down on the stairs outside the saloon. He bowed his head and whispered a little prayer for the horse, then began bawling like a child. The children looking up from their game, watched the man with sympathetic eyes, but the horse, dead where it hit the ground, was wearing a grin as broad as the west itself.

The Great Drink of Compassion

I GO TO THE bar with the moose head that haunts me. I check my thumbs at the door and settle onto a stool. I order the great drink of compassion and cup it in my hands like a squirrel. Suddenly my own humanity overcomes me. I throw myself on the bar and begin weeping like a child. I weep for the moose looking down on me with glass eyes. I weep for the bartender who takes my glass away. I weep for the man in the flannel shirt and for the woman who walks past the window alone. I even weep for the guy with the rough hands and the gold watch who tosses me out on the street. I walk home through the snow with my thumbs in my pockets and a circus bear riding my back.

Scenes from the Field

THE CROWS TAKE OVER. Descend on the field and rape it. Broken stalks frame the ground like chalk outlines. The crows are thorough; comb the mud for every last kernel. They never look up. Forget about the sky. Forget me.

I am the scarecrow locked in traffic. Naked, I stand like a hood ornament peering over the nose of my car. Days pass. Years. When I finally look up I watch the light turn red and pass behind some clouds.

The Lemming Parade

THE APES ARE MULLING about the magazine racks and the rhinoceros are shuffling their feet. Somewhere a building realizes it settled and turns to the bottle. Oh for the lasagna roaster purchased from the gift registry. Oh for the days of dull lawnmower blades. A meerkat and a muskrat are playing pinochle in the park but neither knows the rules, they're just biding time.

The first snowflake settles to the ground. Then another and another. It's not snow, it's confetti. It's tickertape for the Grand Lemming Parade. See how they fill the streets, see how they celebrate. Up the stairwells, onto the roofs, see how they smile right up to the end. Their tiny tails trailing like comets.

Wolf Tickets

ON EVERY STREET THERE is a child. In every city there is a street, and almost always several. On every child there is a sucker or a yo-yo, a baseball card or some other such nonsense, but not always. On every corner there is a wolf. It's the same wolf on every corner. It has always been there. When the people were children it sold them ice cream. Now it's selling tickets to the Greatest Show on Earth. It's the American Dream, it's priced to sell, and people are buying, buying, buying. Lines are forming, every corner, every street, every city. All anyone speaks of is the possibility of an encore.

In the Desert

I AM LOST IN the desert with no water and no company to speak of but a ragged coyote that claims to be my spirit guide. As the sun rises over the endless expanse of sand, I pause in the shadow of a dune to catch my breath. Suddenly the coyote begins circling around me, chanting and waving its arms in the air like a giant stork. "Many years ago," the coyote starts, "this land was covered by a great sea." With this said the coyote pauses and looks about, as if a school of mackerel were passing over our heads. "Now," it continues, "now it's gone but the blue, the cool, ethereal blue remains. It comes out at night and stays until morning when the sun chases it back into the sand. There it sleeps, there it waits for us, just below the surface." With that the coyote drops to its knees and begins digging feverishly into the ground, sending a spray of dust into the air like a tiny tornado trapped in a sandbox. I shake my head and get up, knocking the dirt from my clothes. "Blue," the coyote shrieks over its shoulder as it watches me leave, "blue like the other side of a dream," but I've heard enough. As I make my way over the next dune, I set my sights on a buzzard waving to me like a drunken uncle from a distant cactus.

Ed's Begonias

FOSSIL FUELS FIRE UP the local Bar-BQ joint and sure enough there's Ed, rake in hand. It's raining and Sunday and I can't believe I'm not in Dallas, but I'm not. Sometimes a pork sandwich is all it takes but today I need more. I need cement shoes and an alcoholic halo, rock industries and the kind of grave disappointment you just can't buy anymore. My solution is a fresh siesta, curled up like a pipe-fitter in his mother's sewing box. The rain subsides and Ed reemerges to chase the rabbits from his award-winning flowerbed. Night-crawlers rise up and beach themselves on the lip of the driveway as the mink in the hutch behind the garage chant a Buddhist prayer for peace. Somewhere from my childhood a dog barks.

Stand-off in the Kitchen of the Angry Sun

IT'S ALMOST TOO EARLY for coffee and the sun glares at me as it pulls itself over the windowsill, but I'm happy. I'm making an omelet. I'm standing in the kitchen, whistling in my boxer shorts, and my testicles are swinging in perfect time. It's going to be a great day. It's already a great morning and the first egg I broke was a double yolk. The rest of the eggs are quite normal, as is the milk, and the butter, and just when I reach for an onion to liven things up, three mice appear from behind the toaster. They are dressed like Mexican bandits and they demand my cheese. They have little sombreros, little pistols, and the one in the middle has its whiskers waxed into a handlebar mustache. As I stand there pondering the intricate mechanics of their tiny firearms, they inch across the counter and repeat their demands. No one moves. The only sound is the slow suck of hot water through coffee grains. Just then the toaster goes off and we are all struck by the image of hot toast framed against a window full of angry sun.

Nuclear Winter

WE ARE ON THE brink of nuclear winter and outside the snow-capped grain-silos are poised to launch at the first word from the cow. I decide to hole up in the attic and ride this thing out. It is a mistake. The cats are the first to realize it. They run out into the snow clawing at their eyes. The attic seems colder without them. In the corner of the room a coven of barstools have gathered around an old copper kettle. The mouse that lives inside fancies it a steamboat and patiently awaits its next port of call. The stools too are patient, waiting on the mouse as if for toast. It's a cycle really . . . the stools watching the kettle as I, myself, sit watching the stools . . . the windows staring in at me, unaware of the sunlight slowly warming the kettle . . . and so it goes, and so it goes . . . it's a cycle really.

A wire birdcage hangs from the rafter just above my head. I hook a Christmas ornament on its swing and give it a nudge. In the bulb's reflection I can see a room similar to the one I'm standing in, only this one is entirely red and appears carved from stone in the fashion of a cave. It is inhabited by a hideous creature with loose red skin and long webbed fingers and above it a red Christmas ornament dangles from a dripping stalactite. There is a reflection in this ornament as well and in it I can see a room even smaller than the last. This time it is an attic identical to my own and there is a man inside who bears a great resemblance to me, as a much younger man. He has a full head of hair and seems very confident, strong. It's hard to make out but I think he is wearing a crown on his head, no, it's a birdcage but it has a large ruby resting in it. In the stone's reflection there is yet another room and this last one is very small and very hard to see. There is a coalminer peering through the darkness and the beam of his headlamp has caught something shining above him. It is, of course, another birdcage. Inside this smallest of cages, is a tiny canary. It is a vibrant bird, though no more than a speck of color in the grand scheme of things. The canary is sitting very still on its swing and has a single atom clenched tightly in its beak. The coalminer seems to regard the bird with quiet indifference but the bird has the look of one who knows just enough to be afraid.

The Wolf Union

IT HAD BEEN A long winter. Deer were scarce and morale was low. It seemed a wolf couldn't chase a rabbit without butting heads with a wolverine. Something had to be done. The wolves banded together and formed a union. A meeting was called and all of the animals of the forest were invited. It was a grand affair with much hoopla. One by one the wolves that had been elected to office took the podium and voiced the concerns of their fellow wolves. With each speech the wolves' spirits rose higher and higher. The meeting was a wild success, and afterwards the wolves ate most of the animals in attendance, except the bears and the wolverines. They were busy making plans for their own unions. It had been a long winter.

Wild Night in Urbana, Texas

A GREEN-EYED GECKO in a leisure suit thumbs his way down the road and snags a ride. "I dream in flavors," he says to the trucker, flicking his tongue out to taste the air. It's the prom night of lounge lizards and all across the Lone Star State Gila Monsters are slipping into a second skin of sky-blue tuxedos and neon neckties. A sidewinder sashays into the room on legs fashioned from clay cowboy boots and tips a turquoise sombrero to the skink in the corner. It's a gamble but he's got an El Camino stammering outside, a couple of horse blankets tossed in the trunk and a throb that tells him tonight he's going to score.

Autumn Comes to Sugar Creek

THE TOMATO BOMB IS ticking in the head of a rabbit unaware of the perils of cabbage. To the corn all is right with the garden, only the hush of foliage stooped under its own weight to inspect the occasional root system. Yet somewhere else, somewhere far from this place, it has begun and September spreads across the sky as if across an unmade bed. The chickens know it, feel it as they feel the stones shift in their gizzards after a heavy swallow of rain. The dog lying on the porch knows only that something is missing when it licks at its underbelly. The rabbit knows nothing. It is a live wire buried in the wall. It nibbles at the cabbage without so much as raising an ear at the oblivion and the tomato slowly ticks away from yellow, to pink, to red.

Parking is Free on Weekends

A MAN NOTICES A squirrel scurrying about some leaves in the park. He is suddenly overcome by feelings of love. "It's wrong," cries an old man sitting on a bench nearby. "You must never notice." But it is too late, the man is in love and must now marry the squirrel. The whole town is upset at the man for noticing. "It's a mistake," they repeat to anyone who will listen, but they must prepare for the wedding. The wedding is more of a parade than a ceremony. Children line the streets with baskets of rose petals as the procession makes its way toward the church. "Keep your eyes down," their parents instruct. It is a beautiful summer day, but the people refuse to notice. "It's not right," they shout as the wedding party passes the hardware store and rounds the corner. The groom is upset with himself for noticing the squirrel. "I was wrong," he says over and over again as he makes his way up the steps of the church. The squirrel too is anxious, fidgeting in its cage. "It's not natural," proclaims the minister as he takes his place at the alter. "You must never notice," whispers the best man as he hands over the tiny ring. "It's a mistake," voices ring out from the back of the chapel as the ceremony proceeds. The whole town holds its collective breath as the two exchange vows. "I do," the man says aloud to the squirrel and a woman in the front row actually sheds a tear. "This whole town has gone to hell," proclaims the minister and the organist begins on cue.

Magpies and Orphans

TWO ORPHANS SIT IN a tree cawing and plotting. Two magpies blow overhead like chimney ash. The birds are coalminers peering down at the open mouth of the tree. The children chatter like squirrels shaken in a birdcage. The boys trade punches and name their bruises after the islands they most closely resemble. All bruises are named Cuba. All magpies are orphans.

Two children perch on an electrical wire slung low and limp between its two parental figures. Two magpies shoot marbles in the dirt and eye the leather belt that hums above them. Every so often a cloud belches out another orphan into the air. Soon the sky is full of them. The sun wears their dark bodies like an eyepatch.

Two kids sit on a split rail fence molting. The feathers on their wings have been replaced with gum wrappers and old baseball cards. The orphans stand on a bough arguing over the last apple of summer. The tree bobs beneath the horizon, tethered by the roots that fan out beneath it like ants. The magpies are beginning to understand they may never have a family.

Two birds in flight, making for the dirt road that parts the wheat like a corn snake. Two magpies watch from the dark keyhole already shedding its leaves for the winter. The orphans have a pact; they are never going back. The magpies beat the dust from their feathers and start toward the home. One wrestles with a cowlick as the other struggles to pull on its knickers with its beak. Their black feathers gleam purple in the dying light. Somebody's got to love them.

The Widow

AN OLD WIDOW LIVING alone takes in the unwanted children of the world. Before long her house is bursting at the seams. The children stand shoulder to shoulder in the bedroom, the kitchen and clear down the hallway. In the attic they lay stacked nearly to the rafters. Still the old woman can't bear to turn them away. She begins piling them up behind the woodshed and even hangs a few out on the clothesline. This gives her an even better idea. She begins fastening them to kite string and hangs them out, one by one, in the sky. Higher and higher they go until their pale faces and open mouths are no more than specks against the gray canvas of clouds. She tethers them to the wooden fence running the length of her property and takes special care to notch their names in the wood with her pocket knife. She reels the children in for their birthdays and alternates holidays as best she can. She tries to make sure each child gets a few home cooked meals a year. Sure there are her favorites; Sue has spent more than her fair share of nights beneath a ceiling, while David has nearly been picked apart by the crows. Electrical storms are another concern. Still, the old woman watches over the children faithfully until they are old enough to be set free. The frail, thin bodies found strewn about the neighboring county are legend.

Family

A CHILD WHO ALWAYS gets his way decides he wants to trade places with the family cat. His mother, a widow who hasn't the heart to deny her son's requests, feels she has no choice but to give in. Every morning while her son lies napping at the foot of her bed, she gets up and prepares the cat for school. It isn't fair to the cat, she knows this, but she loves her son so. Time goes by and the cat begins to make a name for itself. It excels in its studies, is a stand-out athlete, and there is talk of a scholarship in its future. The woman is proud; the cat has become a good son, but the boy has gradually slipped further and further into his new life as well. Then one fall, shortly after the cat has gone off to college, the boy slips out the back door and disappears into the alley never to be heard from again. Now the woman is alone. She gets letters from the cat from time to time. It's doing well for itself, and it makes her happy to see what a fine upstanding man the cat has become, but a part of her is always sad. Every night before going to bed she says a prayer of thanks for the son who makes her so proud and leaves a pie pan of milk on the stoop for the son who disappeared into the night.

The Holidays

It was Thanksgiving and the whole clan had just settled into their seats when my mother-in-law took a nasty spill in the kitchen. She was just returning to the table when the toe of her shoe caught the linoleum. I was the first to reach her and it wasn't pretty. She was rolling around on the floor, sobbing hysterically and clutching her hip. "Better have a look, Molly," I said. It didn't look good. Already it was swollen and the purple blooms were a dead give away. "I'm afraid it's broken," I said as my wife fought back tears. "I think we're going to have to put her down." There was a lot of commotion from my wife's side of the table but eventually my brother-in-law brought me my rifle. I loaded carefully; this was no time for mistakes. Just then my mother-in-law jolted up with a start. She looked confused and somewhat desperate. "Please Jon," she said. "I think I can walk on it." I looked down at her. "Molly," I answered, "you know this is probably best for all involved." But she stood up, faltering like a colt. "No," she said. "I'm really much better. I think I'll just head home and lie down for a while." As we settled back at the table I thought of my mother-in-law staggering around in the snow. The injured and the old were always singled out by the pack. I had seen the wolf tracks circling the house that morning. With any luck, it was already over.

Evening Hours

THE MOTHS WERE EATING away at Grandpa. He hadn't aged well and was never packed away properly, but he said he didn't mind. He told us when he was a boy his parents had fed him to the chickens. He said a life without sacrifice wasn't worth living. We patted him on his bald head and took turns kissing him good-night, then shut the door quickly to keep from letting moths in the house.

Dusk Falls on the Kitchen

THE MOUSE HAS MADE off with the cat's ear, leaving a ransom note smeared along the baseboard in cheese. The cat now spends its days sliding along the floorboards with a shot-glass to its temple, listening for sounds of laughter from the crawlspace below. I sit at the kitchen table shooting gin and mourning the loss of my favorite glass. In the mesh of the screen door I trace the outline of raccoons scurrying across the yard. They've been meeting behind the garage, finalizing a plot to block out the sun. The spider in the window above the sink has similar plans. Everyday it weaves another layer of skin over its web, dimming the room to a premature dusk.

Part Two

Trickster in the City

COYOTE LAZY. COYOTE STARING off at something in the distance as the conversation lags and the sky darkens to the match the façade of the Chrysler building. A walk. A walk might be the thing. Coyote leaving. Coyote slipping out without paying the bill. Coyote on the street, the hustle and bob, the easy getaway. Coyote gone. The street is an unpleasing canvas to coyote the artist. Poor light, no color and a complete disregard for balance. Coyote arranges the prostitutes on corners by height and hairstyle. Coyote the artist finding beauty under every rock. Coyote paints all of the cabs of the city yellow. "And that is why the cabs are yellow today," says coyote. "We're the Yellow Cab Company," says the cab driver. "We've always been yellow." Coyote dismissing the cab driver. Coyote hearing, seeing only what coyote wants. Coyote the striped dart fish surveying its neon grotto, ghetto no more. Coyote creator. Coyote savior. Coyote feeling a little bad about the restaurant thing, but not so much anymore.

Trickster on Hajj

DUST CLOUDS AND MOUNTAIN Dew empties. Coyote on the pilgrim trail. Coyote making the journey to Bentonville, Arkansas, holy city and birthplace of Walmart. Coyote in ihram, his slender frame adorned with the sacred plastic bags of Walmart. The same holy bags kept for sack lunches and used to bury the dead. Coyote reverent but also reflective. Coyote remembers how it all started, with just a pair of cut-offs and some pocket change. And now? Millions of pairs of cut-offs, thousands of dollars in change. Coyote but one in a sea of true believers making the spiritual journey from Raleigh, to Nashville, to Little Rock. They will find refuge along the way. The white man in the Nascar hat who hands out sticks of gum in Greensboro. The black woman in Memphis who makes her own beef jerky. Coyote knows we are all the same in the electric eye of Walmart, peering down from above the parking lot. One people united by a love of five dollar patriotic t-shirts and eighty-pound bags of kibble. Coyote the pious adjusts the plastic bag of moon pies slung over his shoulder and hunkers down for the long road ahead.

Trickster at the Writers Colony

FRESH AIR AND CONIFEROUS shade. Coyote takes in his sur-
roundings. Gently rolling hills pocked with cottages, clapboard
legions on an otherwise idyllic view. A symptom concealing
what? Harsh landscape? Undesired geological features? Coyote
stumbles back to this place summer after summer like the B-
movie character returning to the sequel. The only surprise is the
lack of surprise. Coyote the bird born into a religion of migratory
patterns. And now what? Coyote lights a cigarette, stares at the
empty page and waits. The sound is the slap of weathered oilcloth.
The sound is a stain. How to capture that on paper? How to write
a weather, a past? Craft and technique fail here. Urine and sweat
would be too deliberate and awfully hard work. Coyote waiting
on talent as if on puberty. He wears down; eyes sinking, flesh
hardening to leather. He has found his way back to the bronze-
age. And now what? Coyote has retraced an entire history but
still failed to conjure one, small art. But that is something, isn't
it? Why yes, that is something. Congratulations. Congratulations,
Coyote. Congratulations.

Trickster at the Free Clinic

THE SWEET STENCH OF urine and a hypo for every junkie. The circus is in town and Coyote is a kid again. Gone are the days of cotton candy and popcorn, Italians flung to the sawdust. Yet the clowns remain, their numbers swelling as they stream from the men's room as if from a tiny car. In the waiting area an addict climbs onto his seat and prepares for his next dive. He steadies himself against the magazine rack and peers down at the linoleum rippling below. The show has begun and Coyote grabs a seat up front beside an especially gruesome leper. "Pardon me, but could you lend me a hand?" "Mind if I steal your ear for a moment?" "Hey Buddy, is that your dick on the floor?" Coyote enjoying the show, taking in all the sights. The freaks are all sufficiently freakish, though Coyote has a hard time telling the bearded lady from the fat lady as both are bearded and morbidly obese. A nurse emerges from behind a curtain to address the crowd. "Schwebel?" she asks. "Schwebel?" "Two over here," calls Coyote, passing a ten down the row. A page booms out over the loud speaker, "Doctor Ahmad, paging Doctor Ahmad. Doctor Ahmad to obstetrics." Coyote takes his cue and leaps into the spotlight. Coyote spectator no more. Coyote ringmaster, Coyote tophat of the big top working the crowd into a frenzy. "Ladies and Gentleman, the moment you've been waiting for has finally arrived," he announces to the bruised and the bleeding. Coyote splashes through the swinging doors of the delivery ward nearly knocking over a nurse. He turns to face the crowd, bows low at the waist then tears open the medical curtains theatrically. "Ladies and gentleman . . . behold the greatest show on earth!"

Trickster at the Revival

COYOTE GLORIOUS! COYOTE A full-fledged spectacle rivaling the Holy Spirit itself. Coyote staring into the white ceiling of the church tent as if into the face of God, the future . . . a blank canvas. The present . . . a blank check. Coyote slipping into the slurred speech of tongues as if into a warm bath. Coyote allowing his mouth to take on a life of its own, his tongue the snake passed among the pews. Coyote surprising himself with the ease of it all, part yodel, part turkey call and a dollop of childhood nightmare. Coyote allowing himself the full climax of Pentecostal fellatio, even if playing it from the part of the woman . . . faking it all the way. Coyote now rising from the floor, holly roller rolling no more. Coyote reaching out to the congregation, placing hands. Coyote healer. Coyote miracle worker. Coyote humble instrument of God, "And Coyote says let there be light," and Coyote flips on the lights. Coyote becoming that light for the crowd. Coyote lighting the path to salvation, a path to be walked free of the burdens of the material world. Coyote helping his fellow man to lighten the load. Coyote testifying. Coyote calling on God to witness. Coyote praising Coyote. Hallelujah.

The Man Who Killed Polka

"A SKATEBOARD IS THE perfect gift for any occasion," said the man smiling as he shook hands with the well-wisher. Then he placed the skateboard with the others beside the coffin. It was the dawn of the Golden Age of Rock-n-Roll and outside a man with an accordion was drying his eyes on the shirtsleeve of a beat cop. The officer had never really cared for accordions (or accordion players for that matter) but he had once shared a drink with the Prime Minister of Canada in a German dance hall where a polka band was playing. The barmaids were all dressed in lederhosen and wore their hair in long braids but what he remembered most about that day was the precocious little boy at the table beside him. He was riding a skateboard up and down the aisle saying, "one day I will put an end to all of this," and then one day he did.

An American Story

TWO POSSUMS DRESSED AS children (their mother raised them as such) were crying when their father (not a possum) came home. Their mother (not a possum either) was already there. She stayed home with the children everyday and kept house (though actually they lived in a bog swamp). There was a family dog too but it doesn't come up until later (when it dies). Now the mother had sent the children outside to play so she could get some cleaning done (an optimistic thought in a bog swamp). The children sat under a tree and ate the apples that had fallen to the ground (they were rotten). The ripe apples were still hanging from the boughs but the children were not allowed to climb the tree because they hung from their tails (which disturbed their parents to no end). As the children stuffed their mouths with the brown, sticky fruit, their dog, Ernest (a Laplander), bounded across the street to join them and was struck by a car. Now I'd like to tell you the dog died quickly, so I will, but actually it was a long, agonizing death involving hours of grueling pain and convulsions. The children were devastated. They ran into the house bawling, which is how their father found them when he came home (with the money he had stolen from the bank). He was a raccoon and a master thief. He and his accomplice had been planning the heist for weeks. His wife had known nothing about it (although she knew his accomplice all too well). He was a dashing possum with a broad toothy grin and a weakness for tragic women.

The Last Romantic

A MAN HIKES DEEP into the forest to camp out beneath the stars. Sometime in the night a weasel emerges from the woods and makes its way to where the man is sleeping. The weasel begins licking the man's ear, its tongue reaching deeper and deeper into his head until it finally penetrates his dream. The man begins making soft cooing sounds and slowly opens and closes his hands. In his dream, he is being tended to by a beautiful nurse. She is rinsing his ears with a turkey baster and has instructed him to examine himself for signs of a hernia. The woman is very attractive but he can't make out her face because she is wearing a surgical mask. It is both erotic and yet somehow vaguely familiar, like removing the bra of a high school sweetheart to find your own mother's breasts staring back at you. "Everything looks good down here," the man suddenly calls out and the weasel stops licking. In his dream the nurse is just beginning to remove her mask when . . .

The man awakes to find himself face to face with the weasel. At first he is startled, but he soon regains his composure. "It was you?" the man says out loud and the weasel takes a cautious step back. The man stares into the creature's beady little eyes and is surprised to find them warm and inviting. A million thoughts race through his mind; the logistics alone were almost beyond comprehension. "I love you," he decides he wants to say and then he says it: "I love you."

The weasel looks quizzically at the man. Then, without warning, it leans forward and bites down on the man's nose, hard. A piercing shriek erupts from the man's open mouth. He leaps to his feet, arms flailing, and tosses his head from side to side. The weasel digs in. The man begins running around the campfire, shaking the weasel like a rag doll. Finally, he grabs a boot and knocks the creature to the ground where it snarls at him over its shoulder, then disappears into the underbrush.

The next morning the man calls his mother to relay the details of the previous night.

"Well your first wife was a weasel," his mother says sternly, "and you remember how that turned out."

"But this is a different weasel," the man replies. "You don't understand, this is completely different . . . "

Another Lemur, Another Story

THE LEMUR STIRS FROM its sleep, steps onto a limb to peruse the foliage. The zoologist lying beside it awakens with a start, begins groping about the nest for her clothing strewn amongst the branches. The scent of musk lingers on the leaves of the canopy and the woman pauses, remembering the details of the night before. The lemur plucks an orchid from a nearby vine and raises the flower in a sweeping arc before letting it come to rest in her hair. The woman blushes, hides herself playfully behind a Pandanus leaf before letting it fall, along with her clothing, to the forest floor. But this isn't the story of lemurs or the women who love them. This is the story of the little girl who loved that story. And how she cried herself to sleep each night when no one would tell it to her. And how she cried herself to sleep each night when her Father tucked her in.

This is the story of the little girl and her escape to the dark jungles of Madagascar . . . and the lemurs. "Ghosts" the Malagasy called them but the girl wasn't afraid. She would whoop it up with the lemurs in the canopies of the Tapias and Umbrella Palms. Get good and liquored up, start babbling Sinatra to the beat of the Namazaha Falls. Legend had it if you looked an Aye-Aye in the eye, a curse would befall a member of your family, but this only added to its charm for the little girl. She would lose herself for hours in the lemur's blood-red gaze, stirring her martini slowly. The moon would look in on the girl from time to time, and cry its black tears for the child who, at such a tender age, had given her heart to the lemurs. And those tears formed a tar pit beneath her bedroom window where many a beloved neighborhood pet disappeared never to be seen again. And the little girl liked that idea very much and would often place her Mother's diaphragm in the bushes outside her window, but that is another story.

This is the story of the little girl, as told by the moon to the lemurs; perched like dreamy children in the gently rocking tree-tops. And how afterwards, the lemurs would climb to the highest reaches of the baobab trees and howl into the depths of the jungle until watch-fires bloomed in Taolanaro and villages up and down the coast. And how those cries would carry out past the Comoros Islands, out across the dark waters of the Indian Ocean, the Pacific ... out to the little girl. The lemurs were calling for her to join them. Another ghost of the forest haunting the treetops, sending the villagers scrambling at the approach of night. Another swinger in a monkey suit sipping sweet vermouth. Another misplaced child of nature howling at the moon from the crotch of a tree.

Urban Myth

A COUPLE AWAITING THE arrival of their first born delivers instead a ring-tailed lemur. They are beside themselves. The father beats the obstetrician with clenched fists. He curses the nurses and flings himself to the floor bawling. The mother stands up on the table and denounces God. The next day they go home. The lemur eats all of the houseplants and defecates in the sink. It refuses to come down from the refrigerator and keeps them up all night chasing flies along the window screens. The parents are mortified, but being optimistic people they remain patient. They dress the lemur as a boy and name it Colin. They send it to the finest schools and indulge it with every extravagance. Finally their hard work pays off. One morning upon entering the nursery they find a neat stack of money in the lemur's place.

The Same Only Lower

A CITY GROWS UP around a tree where a squirrel makes its home. The city grows larger and larger and soon even the small space occupied by the tree is needed. The squirrel must now leave its home and go off to live in the city. Since squirrels live in trees, the squirrel must now decide to join the ranks of rats or men. The squirrel decides to become a rat, but it does not know how to be a rat. The squirrel sees a man passing by and decides to ask the man. "How does a rat live?" the squirrel asks the man. "I am running late," says the man rushing off to somewhere. "But how does a rat live?" the squirrel asks again. "The same as a man only lower," says the man rushing off to somewhere. So the squirrel rushes off to join the ranks of rats living in the city the same as men only lower. One evening the rat passes under a streetlamp and is reminded of a certain moon that used to hang over a certain tree growing up from its memory. The rat stops and stares up at the light. It wants to climb up into the branches of that memory so as to get a better view of the light, to see if it is indeed the same moon it remembers. But the rat has made its decision and it is too late to turn back.

Poem with Weasels, c. 1930s (Black and White)

TWO WEASELS SETTLE INTO their seats at the back of the movie house and wait for the serial to begin. As the screen crackles to life, they are presented with the image of a weasel as portrayed by a mink. The actor is dressed in a long striped sweater that hugs its slender frame like a sweatsock. It wears a large wool cap pulled down over its beady eyes. As the weasel slinks across the stage, popping in and out of darkened alleys, it is accompanied by an organ playing the ominous theme of the "bad guy". Finally, the creature stops and cranes its long, plastic neck around a corner. Outside the candy store, a child sits alone on a park bench, clutching an oversized lollipop. The weasel licks its whiskers, rubs its hands together like a fly. A clamor of hisses and boos erupt from the audience and the two weasels decide to slip out the exit.

Outside the temperature has dropped noticeably. One of the weasels turns up the collar of its coat and is immediately aware of looking conspicuous. Across the street, a black child sits on a shoeshine box, swinging his legs and smearing shoe polish on his face. He pauses to look at his reflection in a store window, then smiles and dabs on a bit more. An enormous poodle bursts from the gates of the city park, its middle-aged owner in tow. The two are a fantastic spectacle of curls, pearls and mink. The woman frantically flails her shopping bags, trying desperately to keep her footing on four-inch heels, but each new square of concrete finds her closer and closer to disaster. Finally, she is lifted from the pavement like a kite and sent sprawling into the street. A cop appears to help her to her feet, then turns to face the weasels. Slowly the officer approaches, thumping his nightstick like a farmer knocking dirt from a turnip. The weasels stop. The first instinctively drops its eyes to its feet, begins nervously smoothing down its collar. The second hesitates, then cautiously steps forward. With a nod to the officer, it motions over at the young child whose white smile slowly dissolves into his shiny black face.

The Park

THE PARK HAS BECOME a dangerous place, someone is up to no good. An old man ignores the warning signs posted at the gates. He takes his regular seat on a bench and produces a bag of breadcrumbs from his coat. Within minutes they are upon him.

The police find an old wool overcoat lying in a hump beside a park bench. Inside the coat they find a neat pile of bones, the skeleton chewed clean. A few gray teeth lay scattered on the sidewalk nearby. One of officers finds a yellow post-it note stuck to the wooden slats of the bench. The message scrawled on the note reads: *more old men or we start on the children — the squirrels.*

The officers sit down on the bench and scratch their heads. One of them picks up a bag of breadcrumbs lying at his feet; begins tossing them out to the pigeons. After a few minutes he clears his throat, "At least we know who we are dealing with."

"Yeah," replies the other, "squirrels I can handle."

Return to Your Safe Place

A MAN IS BIRD watching in the heart of a forest. As he follows the flight of a Scarlet Tanager he suddenly stops and lets his binoculars fall to his side. A horrible idea has come to nest in the back of his mind. What if he was actually the one being watched? He tries to navigate his way through this new and suffocating wood. Surely birds, especially the species he has observed here in *his* forest, were incapable of operating such complex machinery as a pair of binoculars. Unfortunately, this does little to ease the man's mind. Instead, his thoughts race from birds to the many other animals that inhabit the forest, coming to rest finally on the raccoon. Raccoons have paws like little hands, little black hands capable of using simple tools. His thoughts leap back to his childhood. Once, as a boy, he had watched helplessly as a fat raccoon scurried out of the woods and onto their porch. The creature then clambered into an Adirondack chair, lit his father's favorite pipe and proceeded to blow smoke rings into the air, pausing only to tamp down the pipe and wink at the boy! The man begins to sweat. He begins to feel the weight of their eyes upon him and hears the soft scratches of their pens taking note of his every move. He begins to shake and fumble for his inhaler. He needs something right then, a Nuthatch, a Mudlark, anything.

The Zoo

A MAN SLIPS INTO a darkened alley and presses his back to the wet brick wall. Above him, a ring-tailed lemur pauses on a fire escape — its long striped tail, a question mark. The man breathes hard. His hands are dug deep into his pockets. As the rain returns, a hornbill passes overhead and perches beneath a billboard that advertises a local dating service. The man takes no notice. A door opens, scraping against the concrete.

A woman emerges from a nearby bar with a companion. The lemur is joined on the fire escape by a bonobo and a family of vampire bats. Two giraffes arrange themselves behind a dumpster below. All of them hold their breath along with the man, waiting to see what will happen next. Fortunately, the relationship appears to be a platonic one. The two exchange a quick embrace before parting and the woman makes her way up the sidewalk in the opposite direction of her companion.

The man who is lurking in the alley removes a knife from his jacket. The wet blade glimmers like a fish, and the hornbill nearly swoops down for a closer look. As the woman draws near, the tension builds and the bats beat their leather wings in a sustained drum roll. The lemur drops his popcorn to the grateful giraffes below and the bonobo begins to masturbate. Suddenly, the man springs from the alley and drags the woman back into the shadows like a spider. He slashes open the woman's dress and pushes her face into the damp brick. The man rapes the woman as the animals gape in horror. Afterwards, he throws her to the ground and runs off, leaving the woman to stumble back to the bar for help. The animals are furious. This is not what they paid to see.

The Bible of Lost Pets

A LIZARD SKITS ACROSS the street to the yellow curb, cracks its tail like a bullwhip and shakes the sand from its back. A starving dog already on the corner is playing charades. The dog has no tail and must act out whatever it wants, but bacon is hard and unconditional love, nearly impossible. A man with a prosthetic leg and a lap full of bacon stops his car in the middle of the intersection. An old woman with a ragged tongue licks his windshield clean for a quarter, but the man sees unconditional love smeared on the glass and refuses to pay.

The man and the old woman join the dog and the lizard on the corner. The woman buys the man's bacon for a quarter and kisses the dog open-mouthed. The man with the prosthetic leg jumps like a lion through a ring of fire and the lizard throws sand in the air like confetti. The organ grinder's monkey perches on a parking meter and reads aloud from the bible of lost pets.

The Neighbor's Dog

THE STREETS ARE NO place for little dogs. The rain beating down on the discarded couch, the leather breathing hard. The small eyes of cigarettes blinking in the alley. Tomorrow the junkies will suffer a great defeat; tonight they coo like kept pigeons. A child is a dog if you look hard enough. A dog with a matchbook of fireflies, playing in a field. A dog running with scissors through the pages of its parents' wedding album. I'd like to drape the neighbor's dog in my arms, stand at the crosswalk and wait for the clouds to part. I'd tiptoe gingerly down the glass-laden streets, careful not to pause too long at the butcher's window. I'd be sure to pass the chalk outlines at the feet; fully aware gravity is an absurd landlord. We'd pop into the soda shop for an eggcream, some button-candy (licorice is a drug one licks out of curiosity) and we'd be gone, leaving only the sewer grates to gape in wonder at our passing. The streets are no place for little dogs. Much reeling in of fishhooks from darkened lampposts. Much multiplying of mailboxes when you aren't looking. Beneath every manhole cover sits a man, crouching like a spider. In the air above your forehead, your breath twists like a doll on a shoestring. The streets are no place for little dogs. I place it in the seat beside me and slowly drive away.

The Insomniac Sleepwalking

I AM THE TINY vampire that sleeps in a shoebox and is terrified of oranges. I suck on a plum and pace around my room. I shove the pit into the keyhole of my door and it opens.

The air outside is somber. Leaves stick like islands to the wet pavement. The moon dangles like a lonely testicle whispering pick-up lines to the car tops of the city.

A rat approaches me from an abandon car. It is walking hunched over its hind legs like an old woman. It asks to borrow an egg. I toss it a nickel and it scurries back into the shadows like a child with a secret.

The mannequins in the store window whisper like ventriloquists through the glass. Tell me to play with matches. Tell me to climb inside and light their plastic wigs on fire. Tell me they want to burn, just for me.

Watching Jimmy Die

JIMMY HARDCASTLE FALLS ASLEEP smoking. Within minutes the flames are upon him. A crowd gathers on the sidewalk, watching Jimmy burn down. Jimmy is yelling for someone to bring him an ax. He thinks if he had an ax he could hack off his legs, cut the fire off at the knees, but there is no ax and soon the flames are waist high. The fire department says there is nothing they can do for Jimmy. They say Jimmy wants to burn, they are almost certain of it, and besides, Jimmy is highly flammable. The firemen wear long flame-retardant coats the colors of fire: deep reds and yellows. Jimmy is not flame-retardant and pretty soon there is less and less of Jimmy and more and more of the fire. It is a pitiful thing to watch, Jimmy's dying, and the crowd shuffles their feet as the certainty of his fate becomes apparent. Finally around ten the hotdog vendors show up, a final testament to Jimmy's staying power. Jimmy can barely be seen now as the flames lick at the curls above his ears and leap up to singe his eyebrows. Echoes of "jump" rise from the crowd as the firemen unfurl a parachute but it is a faint-hearted display; there will be no leap to safety. Jimmy is going all the way. Jimmy stands paralyzed, peering over his nose at the crowd below, then retreats deep within himself. In the morning all that will be left is a charred spot on the corner where Jimmy stood.

Guilt Comes to Dinner, Stays for Pie

MY MIGRATORY PATTERNS ARE dissipating into a loose pile of nails. I leap, the bitter end never far-off tasting and wonder at the whistle that follows. The Grand Tetons a last moon velvet to procure the chill autumn air. Oh I've been there, said that before and always ever after. I've seen a big one drop/dump bed-loads of smallers like fowl. Yet I can no longer taste the nectarine Marcel, silly goose (whatever your name is), your station in life eternally productive and almost always Bermuda. How sweet the nightlight is blowing out the last wisp of hair from the forehead of a child. Floppy? Floppy is that you? How bitterly fantastic to swan indoors for a change. My ferret stole hissing, my hat reeling from the alcohol. I am caressing away all responsibility, folding up shop and loosening the tenants. Another year we might have made it, you and I.

The Confession

AN ORPHAN WITH A flea for his only friend crouches in a bathroom stall and coaxes the insect from his tangled hair. As the flea explores the creases of the child's hand, the boy begins pouring his heart out to the tiny bug, until he is weeping openly onto the urine stained tile. Afterwards, the boy feels better. The flea too is content and signals this by biting the child on his soft palm.

After the War

Rice, bourbon, and the company of men, these are the things that will see us through winter, said the General. Then he turned and shuffled back into the closet with his pants around his ankles. He was humming "The Battle Hymn of the Republic" and tightening the leather belt around his neck to adjust the pitch. Once he and his collie, Duchess, were safely inside he bid us good-night and shut the door.

We pitched camp outside the closet. Night fell and we built a little fire on the carpet. After dinner someone told a story about a starving orphan who found a canned ham under his pillow but died before he could get it open. The sound of soft weeping filtered through from behind the door.

We drew straws for the first watch and immediately our man deserted. We drew again and again but each time the soldier simply walked off his post. Finally we ran out of straws and placed our faith in chance and strategically placed land mines. The wind picked up brushing the tops of the scrub pines against the ceiling. Sometime in the night Duchess crept out of the closet and disappeared. In the morning we awoke to the general's humming. It lingered above us, rising and falling, then stopped abruptly.

Part Three

Travels with Bear

I

HIGHWAY 9 WAS ALWAYS my least favorite stretch of road, nothing but run down truckstops and the occasional strip joint. So when I saw the bear standing on the shoulder trying to thumb a ride with its impossibly large paws, I thought, this could be interesting. It was probably stupid, I mean, we've all heard the horror stories. There is an all too real danger in picking up a complete stranger, not to mention the fact that this was a bear. Looking back, I guess it was the element of danger I found so exciting. I had never done anything like that before. I'll admit when I slowed down enough to get a good look at what I was getting myself into, I almost floored it. But in the end, I pulled off into a gravel ditch, reached across the passenger seat and pushed open the door.

II

THE FIRST THING I noticed was the smell. I'd always loved the smell of a pipe, something about tweed and leather bound books, a good roaring fire. When the bear pulled out the pipe and looked over at me, as if asking permission, I remember thinking that this was going to be ok. I remember thinking that this, this was a bear of distinction, a gentleman bear and I'm pretty sure I spent more than a few miles congratulating myself. Then the bear pulled out the dog. Or what was left of the dog or some miserable creature that had, until recently, shared the same general shape as a dog. It could have been a raccoon or a really large cat. I'll never know for sure. All that was left was the rump, a stub of tail and two stiff legs jutting out like sticks from a caramel apple. Again the bear paused and looked over at me before continuing. This time I was not impressed. The next hundred miles went slowly.

III

I LIKE MUSIC, ALL kinds of music. I like rock, country, classical and jazz. I like chant, glam, skiffle and scat. I'll do new rockabilly, ambient industrial, lento violento and Paraguayan polka. I'm eclectic and open to new things. Bear likes the jingle for Yum-Tum Bubblegum.

It all started simply enough. I found a nice blues station, the perfect complement to the approaching sunset. A commercial came on, some annoying song by children extolling the virtues of their favorite gum, "Happy kiddies love some Yum-Tum Bubblegum!" Bear sat bolt upright in its seat. I turned the station. Bear turned it back. I looked over at the bear, reached over and switched it again. Before my hand left the dial I felt the firm grip of a bear paw turning my hand and the knob back, three inch claws inadvertently flipping on the heater in the process. By this time the commercial was over and the bear was not happy. It continued to turn both hand and knob back and forth, back and forth, first slowly, then frantically like a man thrashing about in water for his mother. Finally Bear gave up, let go of my hand and slumped back in its seat. There was an awkward silence broken by the occasional snuffle that could have been a whimper. I stared ahead at the sunset that reminded me more of my bruised wrist than anything else.

IV

IT HAD LONG SINCE gotten dark. The bear had fogged up the windshield craning its neck over the dash to look up at the stars. Suddenly it began grunting and pawing excitedly at the door. Up ahead a sign came into view, a sign for a rundown motor lodge. I looked at the bear, it looked at me. Without saying a word I pulled in. I made to get out of the car but Bear pinned me to my seat with an overdone gesture meant to say hold on. I knew where this was going. Lord knows what was collected in that shaggy coat but a wallet was bound to be on the short lists of things not found there. "I know," I said, "I'll cover it," but Bear wasn't done yet. There was a low snuff, like the assumption was a personal affront. "Really," I said, the weight of its paw had started to cut into my breathing, "I want to, you can pick up the next one." Something in my tone must have pleased the bear because this time I was rewarded with a long wet lick that started beneath the rim of my chin and ended in the outcropping of hair that afterwards set out in a dramatic arc. The smell that lingered told of affections for honey and a liberal predisposition for grooming regions my tongue could never reach. "Don't mention it," I said as I stepped from the car.

V

Taxidermy never really showed up on my radar, didn't even register. I mean, I knew what it was, and like other obscure hobbies I tended to exert more energy avoiding its practitioners than I spent contemplating its existence. To the owners of the "Shangri-La Carriage House Banquet Center and Motor Coach Inn" taxidermy was an art form. To Bear, it was the holocaust.

When I first entered the dark, wood-paneled room I remembered feeling like I was being watched. At first I saw only a pale raisin of a man sitting behind the desk listening to an old radio. The room was stale and his head was partially obscured in a cloud of cigarette smoke. Then, as the smoke began to clear, I became aware of the "other" eyes watching me, the glass eyes. The eyes of the deer, wolf, elk and, yes, bear that stared down at me from the walls. My first thought was that I had stumbled into some sort of Disney meets Käthe Kollwitz exhibit. My second thought was the bear.

VI

THERE ARE SOUNDS NOT meant for human ears. Sounds too high or loud to be healthy or so soft that they can't be discerned. There are other sounds too. Sounds too horrible to hold in one's head for long, like the sound of a loved one crying or the rasp of a death rattle. The sound that came from Bear upon the discovery of the dead "art" was still another kind of sound. There were a few moments when I actually thought the situation could be remedied, a few naïve seconds when I honestly believed things might still be salvaged but that was when the bear had only seen the ground squirrel on the desk and the almost cheerful jackalope propped by the waste can. By the time the bear looked up at the walls I understood quite clearly that there was no hope; not for the old man, not for me, not for anyone. And then I heard it, heard it pierce the darkness like a ray of hope, like pure golden sunshine. From out of the tinny radio on the desk came the commercial for Yum-Tum Bubblegum.

VII

THIRTY SECONDS. I KNEW that was about all I had and that was all I needed. There were images flashing across my mind as I splashed through the door and shot across the parking lot. I could see the Bear standing on its rear haunches, rocking gently as if in a trance. I could see the old man, fumbling beneath his desk, for what? A gun? Medication? All I knew at that moment was that in thirty seconds that jingle was going to end and with it any chance for escape and so I ran. I ran and I drove and I didn't stop until I ran out of gas. I stopped at a little filling station just long enough for coffee and I was back on the road again, putting distance behind me for the sake of distance.

Finally, as the sun peeked into the rear view mirror, I slowed down a little and loosened my grip on the wheel. I reached over and turned on the radio. I found a blues station, the perfect complement to the approaching sunrise.

Texas Takes a Holiday

THE LAWYERS HUDDLE AROUND an empty matchbook, whispering family recipes and swapping draft cards. Dusk falls and a jackrabbit steps from behind the backdrop of a sunset, begins playing a harmonica that sounds suspiciously like a violin. Overhead a blimp looms in the shadows like an ominous thumb. Bobbing amongst the sandbags, it snags on a cactus and thousands of tiny Christmas presents spill from its belly onto the stage below. The coyotes that had congregated around the tree halt the execution and immediately an adult bookstore vanishes from the suburbs. Taking hands, the coyotes pray and in the ensuing moment of silence, the convict slips away to resume his former life as a comic book superhero.

Apocalypse-Boogie

THE WEATHERMAN HAD PREDICTED a storm to end all, fire and brimstone, that sort of thing. So I called my wife, told her to pick up Chinese, and left work early to set up lawn chairs on the roof. The end of the world was coming sooner than anyone had expected and the city was buzzing with anticipation. Everywhere you looked people were doing the apocalypse-boogie; running naked through the streets, bouncing off light-posts, flailing about like decapitated chickens. The cabs had all been toppled over so I had to walk home, but it was a lovely walk. Neighbors I had never met greeted me like a brother, a son, and in one case even a lover as I made my way down the street. Outside my house a drunken busload of lemmings stopped me at the curb to ask directions to the nearest sea cliff and when I made it inside my wife was waiting with a dog. I had always wanted a dog. As we sat on the roof, feet dangling from the lounge chair, our nameless dog licking the last of the chop-suey from the paper carton, I felt like the luckiest man on the face of the earth.

Walking the Bat

AFTER SUFFERING A LIFETIME of disappointment, I resolve to put myself out of my misery. I am making my way toward the Jefferson Street Bridge when a brightly painted shop window catches my eye. It is a store called "Oracle Seeing-Eye Dogs" and the words stenciled on the glass read: *They know where you're going, even if you don't!* I decide to go inside if only to point out the irony.

The man behind the counter looks as if he's heard it all before. He is polite enough, even nods his head from time to time. When I finally finish my lecture on marketing to the blind, he speaks. "Our dogs aren't just for the blind," he says.

"Well who else would they be for?" I ask, somewhat snidely.

"Lots of people," he says. "People who've lost their way or aren't sure where they're going. People like you."

"Well, I don't know what the hell you mean by that," I say turning and storming towards the door.

"All I'm saying is give it a try, Buddy," the man says. "It's not like the bridge is going anywhere."

I select a black dog with a spot of white on its chest, some breed of retriever I believe. As we make our way down the street I remember what the man said as we left: "let the dog lead you; trust it." I close my eyes, grasp the harness with both hands and suddenly we are off. The dog immediately heads for the park where it proceeds to squat in the middle of a children's soccer game. Taking its lead, I drop my trousers and follow suit. "This day is turning out to be full of surprises," I say to the referee, watching in disbelief as we trot off the field. The remainder of the afternoon is a glorious barrage of asses, smells, squirrel chases and garbage. We are flying by the seat of our pants and living life without regret. Things are going great until Checkers (I have become somewhat attached by this point) decides to dart in front of an oncoming beer truck and it is here we part ways. The dog is leveled in a fantastic spectacle of fur, steel and beer, and I head for home humming with the joy of having cheated death.

The day proves to be an unexpected triumph, a celebration of the senses and I spring into bed with the satisfaction of having lived life, for once, to the fullest. Today was an epiphany, a high water mark. Tomorrow: the bridge.

A Perfect World

I FIND MYSELF DRAWN to my neighbor's dog. Each day I find a new excuse to return to the kitchen where I am afforded the best view of the creature, tied to a tree in the adjacent yard. It is a flea-bitten mongrel, neglected to the point of abuse. It is tragic and so, it is painfully beautiful. I can't remember ever seeing a creature more beautiful, more unspeakably alone. I have asked the neighbor on numerous occasions to sell me the dog. He too is a tragic figure. "A companion for my morning walks," I explain but he refuses me each time. "I could never part with that dog," he replies. "It's all I have left of my Esmerelda." I tell my wife of my plots to get the dog. "We could sell the house without telling anybody and make off with the poor thing in the middle of the night," I tell her. She pats me on my bald head and smiles. "I'd hate to think of that poor man all alone," she says. "But what about that poor dog?" I protest. She leans forward and kisses me on the cheek. "Some creatures are meant to suffer," she says, "to remind the rest of us how cruel the world really is." And she's right about that, she is. This is no perfect world. Still, I have a dream. The three of us picking up stakes and heading west. Just me, the dog and the open road. And my wife, my beautiful Esmerelda.

The Good Life

WHENEVER I MAKE LOVE with my wife, an Ivory-billed Wood-pecker perches in the tree outside our bedroom. After I am sure my wife is asleep, I open the window so I can have a word with the bird. The woodpecker inquires about our lovemaking and I ask of its travels to Bayou DeView. It is always a fascinating exchange and I am genuinely saddened by our parting, not know-ing how long it will be until we meet again. Whenever I mastur-bate, a hoary, old dog lumbers up the steps and sprawls out on the bathroom tile beside me. This is usually followed by an awkward silence. It seems we have run out of things to talk about.

Gabby

HE WAS WRITING THE Great American Novel and booked a flight to Canada to do some research. It had started out as an action/adventure/romance but now was more of a self-help manual. It was tentatively titled "How to Make Love to an Angry Wolverine" and he hoped his childhood on a farm and years in the pornography industry would be of some service. As it was, he had never really been good with animals or sex and would end up drawing primarily from his experiences as a boy scout. And so on that fateful day when he rounded the bend of the scenic mountain pass and found himself staring eye to eye with the fierce creature, there was a moment of self doubt; as if he were suddenly surprised to find himself there and the many days of hiking and scavenging about the caribou carcasses had somehow been meant for another purpose. Then the boy scout in him returned and the "can do" spirit took over. He slipped calmly behind the creature, lifted its bushy tail as if looking under a rug and went about his business. Afterward he returned to his cabin to put the encounter to paper but no words would come. The experience had ruined him for all others. He fell into a deep depression and spent the rest of his days in his cabin alone. On clear nights, the wolves would come down from the mountains and sing for him.

The Shaman

AN INUIT SHAMAN FED up with humanity leaves his village and walks into the woods to join nature. He decides he will change himself into a polar bear. To his surprise he finds upon uttering his chant he has become instead a walrus, mortal enemy of all polar bears. Disgruntled, he tries again and this time finds he has become a red fox. Though lovely, a fox was a particularly unfortunate choice considering the season and the number of hunters in the village, so after admiring his coat for a short while he tries again. To his horror he finds this time he has become a salmon. A salmon is a disastrous choice, not only because he has now become the favorite dish of every predator in the land, but also because he is miles from the nearest river or stream. As he lies flopping on the ground, his gills vainly throbbing to find moisture in the cold arctic air, he summons the last of his strength for one final attempt. He becomes a snow leopard and quickly converts to Catholicism. He embraces humanity once again and settles down to write his memoirs from his cage in the Vatican.

Finding Jesus

I AM OFF ON an adventure in search of my cat. I bring along Lucifer, my other cat, who up to this point had been living vicariously through the first. We do not bring the fish (50-gallon aquarium) and here their part of the story comes to a close. We are gone but a short while before we find ourselves hopelessly lost. The woods are a self-cleaning oven for bears. The compass—tool of unimaginable cruelty. A mature sycamore can swallow a human head without disturbing a single squirrel! We survive the Ozarks by our wits alone and somehow claw our way back to civilization. We crash through the dense underbrush and stumble naked and dazed upon a church picnic. I kneel on the grass before a large plastic tub of potato salad. "Salvation is mine, Lucifer," I call out and the congregation breaks into a chorus of hallelujah (wondrous people these Baptists). Lucifer is particularly taken with a parishioner wearing a fruit salad on her head (cherries a bit pink, but plums the color of death itself). Later, over ice-cream sandwiches, the minister offers us a place in the congregation . . . his robe. We decline both, but not before stuffing our cheeks with moon pies, ham salad and whatever else we can get our thankful paws on (a deviled egg is a sin indulged out of habit). We sprawl out on the freshly cut grass like stupefied ground squirrels; the hot July sun our smiling taxidermist. Arkansas met and Arkansas conquered, but still we are no closer to finding Jesus.

At the Nunnery

A LARGE FRANCISCAN DIVES into the icy water and in one graceful, fluid motion snatches the fish between her teeth. Many applaud, a few throw roses. The nuns are the most popular attraction at the aquarium, drawing some thirty to forty thousand spectators annually. The head office was concerned in the beginning that such a conservative display could replace Jangles the beloved sea otter, but the nuns soon put all doubts to rest. With their smart, black habits and divine disposition, these "sisters of the holy trinity" have become the darlings of Darbyville. Though somewhat awkward on land, the nuns are angelic in the water. In the wild they are efficient hunters and their silver crucifixes serve as an effective lure. Glistening and twisting beneath the nuns as they swim, the cross draws in unsuspecting prey for the kill.

A Rabbit for Helga

THE FATHER PACED NERVOUSLY in the waiting room of the abortion clinic. Outside the protesters had all been replaced by extras from a documentary on the Great Depression. They were extremely depressed and mulled about the sidewalk dragging their feet, all but one young man who couldn't get into character. He kept saying, "things are looking up" and "at least it's not raining." Inside all was quiet. The only sounds to be heard were the soft pat of the man's loafers on the tile and the muffled scratches of the nurse's pen as she wrote notes in the margins of her romance novel. Finally the doctor emerged from behind the swinging doors with Helga. She was in a wheelchair and holding a large, steel cage in her lap. "Your wife came through fine," said the doctor, "and the rabbit is as good as new."

The Baby-Killing Factory

IT'S THE GRAND OPENING of the new baby-killing factory and the whole town is nerves. I lean my bicycle against a tree, push my way through the crowd, and slip under the skirt of the stage. Just as the mayor's voice crackles over the loudspeakers, I leap onto the podium, snatch the giant, golden scissors from his hands and in a sweeping, exaggerated motion, slice through the ribbon sending it streaming across the stage. The mayor lunges in desperation, flinging himself at the flapping tails of velvet, but it's too late.

The workers watching from the docks just shake their heads in disgust, muttering to themselves as they toss the shiny, new babies back into the ocean.

Blue

THE MATTRESS IS SOAKED and we're taking on water but no one seems concerned. The Captain is preoccupied with smoking his beard, which just this very day has grown long enough to reach his pipe, and the children are all dead. One might expect an air of defeat on such a macabre vessel as this, yet I still manage a smile: a testament to my wife's sack lunches that I hang under my nose like a shingle. The Captain has a rank odor about him that he attributes to his pipe but, unbeknownst to him, he too will soon expire. I can't say I'll last much longer myself. The mattresses continue to die in droves and flake from the ship like dandruff.

I take a deep breath and fill my lungs with sea air, a half-hearted effort to keep us afloat. "I haven't felt this young since birth," I say to the corpse of a newborn seated beside me. It doesn't respond. I shake its little head like a magic eight ball and peer into its milky eyes for an answer. Inside I see the lights of something like a discotheque and for the first time in a long time I find myself thinking of suede. "Oh if only there had been time for baseball," I say aloud, "we could have both retired on an arm like yours."

A strong wind kicks up and smacks the urine-stained sheet that is our only sail. "We're really moving now," calls the Captain, his head now lost in a thin cloud of smoke. I count the whitecaps racing past and scan the horizon for phantom icebergs, a dolphin, anything that isn't blue.

The Ripple Effect

THE SLEEPY SHARK ROLLS from bed at the sound of the bell: the fisherman's foot ringing in the water. On the pier a young girl purchases a dried apricot from a vendor and rolls its wrinkled skin over her tongue before biting down. Behind tightly drawn curtains, the boy who might have grown up to be her great love (or grocer) succumbs to his illness and orphans his parents, as the shark draws behind a curtain of foam. The girl, grown tired of waiting for her father, disappears into the crowded streets of the village as a bell ringing from the marketplace wakes the sleeping fisherman just in time to reel in his apricot. The young boy watching from the pier bites his tongue at the sight of the wrinkled skin. Succumbing to his illness, he runs off to the grocer as if to his lover. The young girl, running late for dinner, stops off at the marketplace on her way home. She purchases a shark from the vendor and leads it home through the crowded streets of the village to meet her parents. The girl is an orphan but it doesn't matter. There are wedding bells ringing in her ears. They're in love.

Crossing the Equator

CLOUDS CHURN ON THE ceiling and the chickens grow restless. For my part, I reach for my hat. I saw this coming. Yesterday the cows were lowing and kneeling on the carpet (the pile may never fully recover). Today, I had an epiphany. "When you get down to it, I'm charcoal," I say aloud. I feel like I could disappear and recompose as a leaf. Ravenous dust-bunnies spring from under the couch and circle my head like magpies. I try counting sheep backward in an effort to wake up, but this annoys them and they turn on me. Armed only with a shrimp fork and my own feeble definition of "domestic partners," I resolve to ride out this storm from the comfort of my bedroom.

I tiptoe past the glacier as it wilts on the sill. Tomorrow it will form the lake I mistook for tears, back in the days when otters were foolhardy. I am crossing this deluge by matchstick, by crocodile . . . I can't even see my feet! I feel like Noah, my many vices hanging from my neck like a beard. Two by two my fears return to me. Some take the form of animals, others my own inadequacies. A dark and bristly pelvis is lurking in the backyard. "Beware," cries the mouse that lives in the kitchen. It is standing on top of the refrigerator, waving a hairy fist in the air and pretending not to be intimidated by the crown-molding. Hand in hand the children of my third-grade class walk up the plank of my ark bearing gifts of wildflowers, while in the bathroom pedophiles wash up for dinner. From the parlor I catch the faint murmur of harpies calling to me from a distant pay phone.

"All aboard the crazy ship," calls our captain, a wolf and former train conductor. It knows nothing of seafaring etiquette but is well versed in railroad jargon. Oh train of ill-guided intentions, it was more than the stray stone that leapt me from your tracks and found me here, aboard this ship. All things creepy contained within its hull. Something about my cabin doesn't sit well with me. The props are right: plastic shackles, scented tea lights, and an oil painting of a shrew beheading a toll bridge. Cigarette jockeys trample overhead as they lead their beloved to befuddled glue. "'Tis a better place," they whisper to velvet ears, "a pane-less view of a much darker viewing box." I say let us don our sleeping caps and pretend to dream but the stable erupts in a unanimous nay.

Time for a visit from Uncle Specter and all the glowworms are present and accounted for. Blind rodents infest my thoughts like children with an ear for candy (A lively bunch of corpses, their mother was a dragonfly). Oh sacred chipmunk, won't you hike up your robes so that I might paint your toenails in the blasphemy of the moment? I toss a silver dollar at your shining utopia and drape a shower curtain over your watchful eye. I blink three times and tie a short piece of string around a short piece of string.

Pulling Taffy

A MAN MAKES HIS way home down the same road he takes everyday. As he drives he notices a groundhog standing in the grass near the shoulder. He drives on and a few minutes later he passes another groundhog, then another. This gets the man to thinking about groundhogs, not the creatures themselves really, but the lives they lead. Up the road the man sees a groundhog standing off to the side, where the pavement gives way to a gravel washout. He pulls his car over. The man gets out and walks around to where the little groundhog is standing. He feels as if he has just stepped from the rain into his Mother's kitchen. The man fumbles in his pocket for the keys he just placed there. He hands them to the groundhog.

"Thank you sir," the groundhog replies. "Now go ahead inside, we have been expecting you." The man looks out into the tiny meadow running alongside the road. In the distance he can just make out the entrance of a hole hidden amongst the weeds.

"Please sir," the groundhog continues. "Go ahead and enjoy yourself. I'll see to your car." The man stands there. He feels himself begin to sway as he follows the Goldenrod and Ragweed with his eyes. He squints at the hole, half hidden by the shuffling grass. He begins to hear music, just barely audible over the rush of passing traffic. It is calliope music and as he listens to it rising and falling on the breeze, he catches himself beginning to follow it across the meadow. He begins to shake.

"I can't," the man cries and snatches his keys from the groundhog. He returns to his car, secures his safety belt and speeds away. Later that evening, he recounts the encounter to his wife.

". . . and when I pulled over to look at the creature," the man continues, "I found it wasn't a groundhog at all. It was an old lawn ornament someone had abandoned on the side of the road. The paint had worn away and it was the chipping that made its eyes look so real."

"But you still haven't explained why you pulled over in the first place," says his wife.

"You should have seen it," the man continues. "It looked so real . . . "

" . . . but if you thought it was real," his wife interrupts, "then why did you . . . "

" . . . and I swear as I pulled away it waved goodbye."

The Deer

I WAS WEEDING IN my garden when a deer stepped out from behind some honeysuckle. It was no more than two feet tall! Even more amazing, it was a full grown stag, complete with antlers. I stood there dumb as the deer approached like a neighborhood cat. I was afraid to touch it; it wasn't of this world or at least not of my world. I looked into its tiny eyes and then for some reason I felt reassured, as if touching this deer was not only completely natural but the right thing to do. I ran my hand down the deer's neck. I stroked its back for what seemed like hours. Finally I picked it up and brought it into the house to show my wife. When she saw the deer she frowned and sat down at the kitchen table. She was silent for a good five minutes before she finally spoke. "You'll have to get rid of it," she said. "And wait until night. We have a baby now; we can't afford to be known as the people who found the miniature deer. Notoriety is bad for children." I waited until sundown to leave with the deer. I drove deep into the country, past the farmhouses with their empty porches, beyond the tentacles of the telephone company and down the evolutionary scale from asphalt to gravel to dirt. Finally I came to a small forest with a stream trickling into it. I got out of the car and took the deer from the blanket I had swaddled it in. "Now you watch out for those miniature wolves," I said, "and for that matter, watch out for the big ones too." I sat the deer on the ground, it seemed to understand perfectly. It licked my hand and calmly walked into the woods. As I drove home I thought of my son asleep in his crib. The things I would teach him, the things he would never know.

The Neighborhood

THE NEIGHBORS NEXT DOOR keep tigers. They have a makeshift cage in their back yard made of steel, wood and chain link fence. The whole thing looks pretty risky, a slipshod version of the pens zoos go to great lengths to hide from the public. The whole neighborhood is on pins and needles about the tigers. People complain incessantly but the couple have a permit, so we assume they know what they're doing. On warm summer nights the tigers' roaring can be heard for blocks. The hair on the back of my neck stands on end as I lie in bed listening to them, imagining them pacing back and forth behind the wooden fence. On sunny afternoons as my son and daughter swing on their playset, I sit atop the slide with a double-barrel shotgun resting on my lap. It's no way to live. Then, just like that, the tigers disappear. Word has it the neighbors grew tired of the hassle and gave them away to a wildlife sanctuary, but no one knows for sure. The pen has been dismantled and the woman has begun planting a flower bed in the corner where the tigers held court. Overnight our neighborhood returns to the quiet life it enjoyed before the tigers' arrival. People aren't afraid to venture outdoors and we're all sleeping like babies. Everyone seems delighted to live, once again, on a plain-old, ordinary street. So ordinary, in fact, that things are beginning to get a bit dull.

One day, I'm doing some weeding around the house when I see Bill Stewart walking up my drive. Bill lives a few houses down. We have known each other for years, though I haven't seen him out much lately. Bill walks over to where I'm sitting on the grass and stops. He has this stupefied look about him, as if he has just seen a ghost and his life is suddenly better for having seen it. "What have you been up to, Bill?" I ask. "Haven't seen you around in awhile." "Been tinkering in my basement," he says, the strange look never leaving his face. Then he leans over and whispers, "Come around the side with me a minute, I got something I want to show you." I get up and follow Bill around the corner to a shady spot beside the garage. Then Bill stops, turns to face me and slowly lifts up his sweatshirt. Underneath is one of the nastiest wounds I've ever seen: four long gashes cutting sideways across his chest, held together loosely with toilet paper and medical tape and soaked through with blood. I look at Bill. "That looks pretty fresh," I say. Bill smiles and nods his head. "In your basement?" I say and Bill nods his head again and continues smiling. "That's beautiful, Bill," I say, barely able to contain my excitement. "Beautiful!"

Inside

OUTSIDE THE CARS HURL themselves at each other, heaping up like cigarettes in an ashtray until even the weasel, greased from head to tail, would turn a pale claustrophobe at the thought of wriggling through the wreckage. No, we prefer to remain indoors, the weasel and I. The calm reassurance of the living room with its soothing earth tones and matching furniture. The sanctity of the kitchen with its religion of delicately placed flatware. It's peaceful here . . . the cows grazing lazily on the plush shag carpet . . . the mouse percolating in the coffee cup.

The Secret Lepidopterist Society

A DOG SNIFFS AT its underbelly, lifts its head, eyes wild with amazement, and bounds off after a butterfly. A man standing nearby watches the dog; thumbs at his own belly through his shirt.

The man goes home. He climbs the stairs to his bedroom and closes the door. The man undresses in the darkness: first his shirt, then his trousers, a sock . . . he raises his undershirt like a veil and stares into the pale face of his belly.

The man sniffs at his belly. He can't smell anything. The man arches his back like a mongoose and dives at the gaping mouth of his navel. The man smells deodorant and later, his sweat overcoming it. The man cannot smell his belly.

The man lifts his head, eyes wild with amazement. He understands now. The man stands up on his bed and howls with delight. He begins running around the room, a naked figure stumbling over phone cords, scaling the dresser. It's so clear to him now. He wonders how he had not seen it there before, fluttering above him in the darkness.

Fate Takes the Scenic Route

ARTHUR WAS ON HIS way home from work when he saw something he had never seen before. There, on Third St. hovering above the street vendors and prostitutes, was a new billboard. It was an advertisement for a perfume called "Solipsist" and the slogan read, "Experience It For Yourself." The ad depicted a beautiful woman standing in what appeared to be a rainforest, baring the obligatory amount of skin and raising a tiny bottle of perfume as if returning it to a bird's nest. But it was the animal staring down from the tree above that caught Arthur's eye. The creature barely existed within the frame of view but its presence had an immediate impact on Arthur. It resembled a small dog with its pointed snout, though it was more like a cat in build. But the truly distinguishing characteristic was the animal's tail: alternating bands of black and white nearly three times the creature's length. The tail rose out of view then returned several feet over where it dangled above the woman's shoulder like a penis at the urinal. It was unlike anything Arthur had seen before and it unnerved him a bit to think such creatures existed without his knowing it.

The image of the creature had a lasting effect on Arthur. It stayed with him through the night and into the next day. At work, he spent his lunch hour searching for the animal on his computer. Finally he found what he had been looking for. The image on the screen read: *lemur catta*, ringtailed lemur, and went on to talk of Madagascar, their diet, gestation period, etc. Arthur was spellbound. As he read, he feebly scrambled to picture what he was reading but his limited knowledge of the world outside the city left him frustrated. Arthur left work earlier and took to walking the streets, his mind clouded with questions he could not answer. What did a lemur smell like? Did they love? Hours went by. Night fell and Arthur found himself in the park, standing at the gates of the city zoo. He had only been looking for an unoccupied bench, someplace to rest his legs, but there he was. A guard was standing near the entrance smoking a cigarette and staring into an open window across the street. Arthur approached.

"You have any lemurs in there?" Arthur asked.

"What?" the guard replied, somewhat startled.

"Lemurs," said Arthur. "They're Prosimians."

"Beats me," replied the guard, somewhat annoyed. "We got lots of animals in there." Arthur looked past the guard. In the shadowy distance he could just make out the silvery outline of cages and every so often a strange cry would emanate from behind the brick wall. Arthur didn't know what was behind that wall but he knew he was getting close, close to something.

"Mind if I look?" Arthur asked. The guard dropped his cigarette on the ground and rubbed the butt into the concrete with his boot.

"I can't let you in here," the guard replied. "We're closed and besides, this zoo ain't free." Arthur just stood there, then quickly fumbled for his wallet.

"Look," he said. "I got one hundred and forty dollars. Will you let me in for that?" The guard said nothing but immediately took the bills from Arthur's hand and swung open the steel gate.

"Don't try anything funny in there," the guard said sternly. "We got cameras." Arthur peered into the darkness looming beyond the gate. Then he nodded to the guard, slipped through the turnstile and disappeared into the night and his new life.

Laurie's House

THE SEA OTTER STROKES its beard and flies in through the window to peruse the toiletries. "I like deodorant," offers Laurie, but the otter pays no attention. Laurie doesn't mind, her doors are open to all creatures, hers is a house built of love, love and that pale, pink stucco that draws the flamingos back each year. The penguins downstairs in the freezer feel naked without their iceberg. Laurie pins a loud Hawaiian cummerbund on a penguin she knows can pull it off and it stands in front of the mirror as if held in a trance. Laurie is always mindful of the mirror and tiptoes past it so as not to disturb its reflection. She did, however, throw a shoe through the television set once. The seven years that followed were the happiest of her life.

The Man from Texarkana

THE COWBOY STEPPED OUT of the saloon, spat on the ground, and looked out over the sleepy, little town. It was time for him to be moving on. The streets were safe, the children were fed, and there hadn't been a grizzly in these parts in years. Still, it wouldn't be easy leaving. They'd have to find a new sheriff, for one thing, that was never easy, and then there was poor Rosalita. Poor, sweet Rosalita, her body laid to rest in the town cemetery. Her memory would haunt him for the rest of his days and . . . but wait, here came Rosalita now! She wasn't dead at all, she had been at the cleaners and was returning home for dinner. She walked up the stoop, handed him his work clothes, and mumbled something about him picking up a pizza, but the cowboy didn't hear a word of it. "Well, I guess my work here is about done," he said, and with that, tipped his hat to the woman retrieving her paper from the curb, mounted his bicycle, and rode off down the sidewalk and into the sunset.

Printed in the United Kingdom by
Lightning Source UK Ltd., Milton Keynes
140938UK00001B/3/P